naked: poems inspired by remarkable women

New Women's Voices Series, No. 162

poems by

Jennifer L. Gauthier

Finishing Line Press
Georgetown, Kentucky

naked: poems inspired by remarkable women

New Women's Voices Series, No. 162

Copyright © 2021 by Jennifer L. Gauthier
ISBN 978-1-64662-690-8 First Edition
All rights reserved under International and Pan-American Copyright Conventions. No part of this book may be reproduced in any manner whatsoever without written permission from the publisher, except in the case of brief quotations embodied in critical articles and reviews.

ACKNOWLEDGMENTS

Naked ~ *HEAT: Nightingale and Sparrow,* Issue 3, June 2019
When Young Girls Dream of Flight ~ as "Poem for Amelia" in *The Bookends Review,* 9/21/2020
Lady Photographer in Chatham County, NC ~ *Just Place* chapbook: https://www.justplace.us/chapbook
Nail Polish Pollock ~ *HerWords: a literary magazine for, by, and about women,* Summer 2020
12 things I wish someone had told me before I gave birth ~ in *Little Somethings Press,* Issue 3, 2021

Publisher: Leah Huete de Maines
Editor: Christen Kincaid
Cover Art: Cameo J. Hoyle
Author Photo: Eric Edward Schrader
Cover Design: Elizabeth Maines McCleavy

Order online: www.finishinglinepress.com
also available on amazon.com

Author inquiries and mail orders:
Finishing Line Press
PO Box 1626
Georgetown, Kentucky 40324
USA

Table of Contents

Foreword 1

Naked 3

Dear Lucy— 4

The Birth of Celebrity 6

Mrs. Kathleen Rance Refuses to Knit 7

General Jones Flies for Suffrage 9

Come Let Us Reason Together 11

When Young Girls Dream of Flight 12

Empty Churches in Oxford 13

One out of four 14

October 26, heavy cloud, low ceiling 16

Lady Photographer in Chatham County, NC 18

Poem from the Petersburg Jail 19

"The Sure Cure for Anti- 21

And all because she wouldn't wash her hair 23

Nail Polish Pollock 25

12 things I wish someone had told me before I gave birth 26

*For my grandmother and my mother
—remarkable women who inspired me.*

Foreword

This collection of poems was inspired by women throughout history who have acted boldly and bravely to make positive change in the world. Some are historical personages who have been forgotten, ignored or written out of the historical record. Others are women I know who have inspired me throughout my life. And finally, some are fictional characters who fought their way out of my brain and onto the page to stake their claim in this collection.

All are women whose passionate and abiding commitment to social justice defines them. Whether they are artists, teachers, lawyers, scientists, mothers, sisters, or daughters, their actions demonstrate their selfless quest to right wrongs.

They are resilient. They are rebels. Each of these women refused to be limited by existing beliefs, ideas and values. Instead they used their wits, humor, courage, and strength to stand up to powerful people and institutions, convinced that they could make a difference.

And they did.

August 18, 2020 was the 100th anniversary of the ratification of the nineteenth amendment to the United States Constitution, which stated that the right of citizens to vote "shall not be denied or abridged by the United States or by any state on account of sex." In the years leading up to this historic change, women from different backgrounds fought alongside their male comrades to advocate for equal rights. Since the Seneca Falls Convention in July of 1848 movement for women's rights has been a protracted battle ranging across the USA and around the world. The passage of the 19th amendment by the U.S. Congress guaranteed women who were citizens the right to vote in America, but left out many non-white, working class and immigrant women.

Voting rights were a huge accomplishment, but they were not the panacea to improve the daily lives of women. Still today, equal access to voting is not guaranteed and indeed, is at risk in many places in America. Early suffrage activists defied society's norms and challenged expectations, setting a new course for marginalized populations everywhere. Post-1920 the struggle continues, for equal access to education, employment, opportunities and most importantly, safety and respect.

Actual and fictional, the women of this collection exemplify this fight. I hope these poems, and the remarkable women they celebrate, inspire, intrigue and inform you, and perhaps encourage you to follow in their footsteps to be brave and bold and to change the world! We still have a long way to go if we want to see all people free.

Naked
>   *(for the women of Salem)*

Naked lately—
flayed over fire
innards exposed indisposed
to tell my secrets
to those who wait.

Called to testify amplify verify the very part
that hides itself away inside.
Bartholomew knew the fate that
I can't escape
To skin the truth off the lies to try
To skim the oil from the water
As it slews in circles across the surface.

Roiling, my brain buzzes with bitter words
Biting back the worst when they threaten to slip through the slit
That gapes in my face.

Naked later—
Stuffed with stones sinking
Into the dank underbelly of the stream
screaming through the current wetly
with a witch's wail.

Dear Lucy—
    (for Sophia Jex-Blake and the Edinburgh Seven)

Back here in Scotland
I can't forget the freshly-scoured rooms and white-washed halls of your hospital in Boston.
Your bravery surpasses any I have seen,
be it in male or female form.

The streets of Cambridge haunt my dreams,
flanked by grand monuments to Athena.
I seek her guidance in this battle,
with naught to defend myself but humble dignity and a quick mind.

To be told "There is no provision" does not deter me.
Would that I could have stayed to press my case,
but father faltered.

Pulled back by the familial cord,
in Edinburgh the winter afternoons weigh me down.
Nor'Loch's stench lingers in the air above Princess Gardens,
and the gaping pit they've dug for the railway swallows the sun.

With your words in my mind I push on,
seeking comfort in the wisdom of those who went before:
Metrodora, Hildegarde, and Trota of Salerno.

Six comrades by my side, we topple the idols,
tear down the gates,
and enter victorious to make our Hippocratic pledge.

Only to be turned away,
scorned and pelted with mud and rubbish.
What is to fear of seven ladies, armed with books?

To heal is a noble pursuit, full of honour and grace.
We will follow in the footsteps of our sister, Agnodice,
who soothed the pain of her sisters.

If they would give us but a fair field and no favour, they would have no regret.

To serve those who suffer is a grand thing, is it not?

Your faithful pupil,
Sophia

The Birth of Celebrity

When Sarah Bernhardt played Hamlet
the audience went wild.
Golden voice and ample bosom,
undaunted by precedent or propriety.

With a scull given to her by Victor Hugo,
she soliloquized as well as Barrymore would,
predicted Gielgud's grace,
foreshadowed Olivier's gloom.

In the duel with Laertes, she thrust her sword vigorously
and flaunted her victory,
proclaiming her place in the pantheon of performers
who dared take on the Dane.

Talent, tall tales and a taint of impropriety
catapulted her to stardom.
Exotic, blustering, strutting on stages from London to Rio
soaking up adulation and applause like sunshine.

When Sarah Bernhardt died,
throngs of mourners filled the streets.
Paris paused as the cortège passed through.
Weeping deeply, a bearded man attended the carriage,
the body within draped in white satin, a silken slipper on lifeless foot.

At Père Lachaise, she was laid to rest in the family crypt,
Division 44, marked with a small stone arch.
They say her menagerie went to the Paris zoo.
Her Andean wildcat and boa constrictor lived out their remaining days,
exotic, blustering, strutting in cages for her loyal fans.

Mrs. Kathleen Rance Refuses to Knit

With trinkets, baubles and bits glowing in the candlelight,
the scent of mince pie enveloped the crowd
at the Christmas Bazaar, 1937.

Children clutched their pennies, hands clammy with anticipation,
eyes searching each table for just the right gift.
The hall echoed with their joyful shouts,
and parents failed to quell their exuberance.

Cider, mulled wine and holiday cheer banished the fear that clung daily
to all gathered
and muted the envy of some.

The Mayoress mounted the dais
wearing a red scarf and matching cloche.
She handed her glass to her husband,
ever the helpful mate.

I'll darn no socks for war, she said.

All of Woolwich stood aghast
(and her husband sighed).
Silence spread across the floor,
like a seeping stain drenching the hall.

I'm not against knitting in principle, though I can't purl or slip, she confessed.
But, I'll not stand by another day as innocent boys are lost.
God, Queen, nor country, no cause is noble enough.

The parents in the crowd gave pause,
the Arsenal workers wilted,
as she met their eyes one by one—
in the stifling heat of that hall.

Snow fell outside, as usual, on our little town.
Joseph and Mary still cradled Jesus in the manger
while sheep and cows stood by.

With less than a fortnight to Christmas Day,
each goose was still carefree.
But plum puddings lurked in the back of each mind.

If Santa came as usual
who would ask for peace
instead of gifts?
she asked.
Hearing no reply,
she took her leave.

Stockings hung, candles snuffed,
the Mayoress and her husband retired to sleep,
while visions of Hurricanes danced in their heads.

General Jones Flies for Suffrage

For fifteen minutes that day I was queen of the sky,
a latter-day Amelia, just as bold and high,
far from the earth, but triumphant and blessed.
The crowd looked so small, no bigger than ants
one and all and I wondered
how they can persist in their thinking
that women are meant for nothing but kitchens.

The hat on my head nearly blew from its perch as
the wind swirled around me and
searching the horizon line, I saw arms outstretched,
voices raised in a cheer, though I was so high
I could hardly hear their praise
mixed with awe and scorn (from the men
who think it wrong for a woman to fly).

But throngs of the faithful, united in mind,
gather round the Wright bi-plane.
And back on the ground, light-headed and breathless—
I look for my parents, I doubted they'd come,
our row over breakfast still fresh in my head:
father was silent, mother said she thought
it scandalous, showy and common.

Later it seems they relented a bit and set out too late.
When the tire took a hit, they stopped
to inflate it, as I soared overhead
or at least I imagined them way down below,
as tiny as ants, who matter as much,
who care not for politics, ethics and such,
they don't fight for justice or stray from the pack.

But instead spend their days marching behind
the rest of the horde in strictly straight
lines, toting the crumbs they've found in the grass,
silently working, like the rest of the class with
heads down and pencils scratching away.

I'll not march in line, nor blindly adhere to the
rules someone else made
I take the lead clear, the head of the army,
with banners and leaflets,
I'll fight for the cause 'til I've no fight left.

They ask about nerves, well, what could I say?
Who wouldn't be nervous, my life is at stake,
but I smile and admit to nary a twinge,
(the wind had me rattled, but I steady
my voice, vouchsafe no fear).

I wave to the crowd and they send up a
cheer, then the top-hatted men, with mustachioed sneers
nervously smile, betraying their worry that
women will win, universal suffrage will come
and we will finally be peers.

Come Let Us Reason Together
(for Inez Milholland)

Inez rode a white horse that day
her prancing steed leading the ladies,
bearing banners demanding their say.

Inez wore a white gown that flowed down
over the horse's flanks
and billowed behind her.

All heads turned as she cut through the crowd
and loud insults, chin held high with one arm raised
to salute the marching multitudes:

wives who left ovens untended and
mothers who shouldered their babes,
sisters who shouted louder than others and
daughters fresh from the factory floor.

A few brothers and sons joined in,
swept up in the general mood of the day.

But most husbands stayed home as
Inez rode her white horse to victory,
smiling all the way.

When Young Girls Dream of Flight

Are those your bones Amelia?
Humerus radius tibia.

If they could speak what stories would they tell?
How you crawled through fire to save Fred Noonan?
How you were cast away like Robinson Crusoe?
Was Fred your man Friday?

About the sun, sharp and relentless, how it burned your skin, already charred?
About the rain that drenched your shelter, hastily built in the shade of a ren tree?

They say you lived for sixty-one days.
Did you live or just survive?
Were you sad or secretly relieved to be free of photographers' flashing bulbs
and Lucky Strike?

Did Fred smoke as the plane plummeted,
cinders mixed with the flaming wreckage?

Benedictine, a shoe, and freckle cream,
remnants of a life cut short.
Called to tell the tale, they will testify to your courage.

The island holds the secrets of your fate.
Like Electra, will you have your revenge
or return to the sky in a play of light?

Goddess of the skies,
Icarus redeemed,
your flame still burns bright
when young girls dream of flight.

Empty Churches in Oxford

Reverend Thorne mounted the pulpit, cleared his throat
and gazed out into the sanctuary.
Sensing something strange, but with expectant eyes upon him,
he launched into his sermon.

Preaching from Psalms, he offered a meditation on peace,
and all in attendance acquiesced.
When he finished speaking, it dawned on him:
not one of his listeners that day was female.

No veils, no gloves, no graceful gestures did he see.
Row after row of suits and ties and freshly-shaven cheeks,
an army of gray greeted his glance.

Exiting the service, a young man pressed a note into the minister's
hand, dipping his head with apparent shame.
Reverend Thorne read three lines engraved therein,
written on fine paper in a neat hand:

"Empty praise of peace in violent times
can no longer be tolerated.
We have pledged to stay away until all thoughts of war are banished."

One out of four
(for Annie Waller)

Mrs. Waller waited for one out of every four,
stooped and fretting,
purple hands twisting in her apron, worn out with
washing.

One out of every four
of all we planted
      sowed
      tended
      harvested
      dried and bagged.

One out of every four we eked out
of this dry and scrubby patch of Virginia clay.

One out of every four comes to us:
stored in our barn, under our roof
for the winter
for the cows
for the bread
for the johnnycakes
for the horse
for the chickens.

Pulled back to Gretna
by family pride,
Odell wants to work it out,
for his mother.

But fate intervenes,
the weapon drawn,
it cannot be sheathed.

None out of every four
black men chosen for a jury,
the planters—white men—
sit in judgment.

With Oscar Davis in the ground
stilled in a pine box
surrounded by his precious earth
forever.

Without change,
one out of every three
black boys will end up in prison,
walking Odell's path.

October 26, heavy cloud, low ceiling
For Gertrude "Tommy" Tompkins Silver

This morning I slipped my gold wedding band
off my ring finger and stowed it in the drawer
next to the bed. Henry slept as I left the house
for the airfield.

Six machine guns loaded.
Mustang's canopy is stuck.
Take-off delayed.

3:30 pm
Repaired canopy, fuel tank full
Destination: Palm Springs, CA; Newark, NJ

Dorothy took off first, climbing up
into the fog
and banking west over the mountains.
> *Halibut weren't biting. I was dreaming about flying.*
> *To rise above the pier, goodbye to the ground,*
> *I become a bird spreading my wings.*

Control tower gives the go-ahead. I ride her
high, into the clouds. Imagine the earth falling
away below, then the Santa Ana peaks loom
on my left. Pull back the stick and feel
her weight shift.
> *Eyes to the sky, I watched the Mustang rise up,*
> *flashing silver like a twisting lure.*

> *Then it spun into the fog. Lost sight of her. But the*
> *sound wasn't right. Coughing, sputtering.*

Imagine my parents and Henry, proudly
grinning while a General presents the medal,
the WASP buzzing with pride.

> *I drop the pole, leap on the railing, lunge out over
> the sea to get a better look. Nothing.*

> *I scream. I shout. Wave my cap in the air and point
> into the ocean. Nothing.*

Assemble your teams and
ready your boats—
my body awaits
along with the wreckage
here in the playground of jellyfish.

It cured her stutter, they say: when she sat in the cockpit her fears fell away and soaring with confidence she flew. She lived in the wind and the sand, with her eyes on the stars.

Lady Photographer in Chatham County, NC
(for Dorothea Lange)

Flanked by dusty roads and scrubby grass
I lug the big box across sun-baked yards,
past a gaggle of wide-eyed kids smudged with red clay.

They gather round, pushing for a better view of the black monster
jostling each other, jolting my plates.

I ask them to resume their hopscotch in the dirt.
As the mid-summer sun beats down a crushing heat
the kids pretend not to notice,
practicing a kind of fortitude
bred into the daughters and sons of farmers
who persevere despite nature's cruelty.

In this fleeting moment I capture their innocence
unbeknownst to them
as they toss the rock and hop
until the sun dips below the Chestnut oaks.

Poem from the Petersburg Jail
(for Pauli Murray)

A ham sits on the good china,
bathed in honey.
Brown sugar yams piled in a bowl
and collards too, dotted with crispy bacon chunks:
an Easter feast fit for a king.

Pies in the icebox—sweet potato and apple—await.
Aunt Sally's whipped a fresh cream

and I sit in the Petersburg jail.

Mac and I disturbed the peace.
We were a disturbance disturbed by the illogical rules of order
on the Greyhound bus,
its broken cushions like gaping wounds.

In this cell among ladies of the night,
of violent day,
of pain and fear,
we feast on their stories and swallow ours.

I would bring them to sit around the mahogany table.
Aunt Pauline would fuss and fawn,
while Aunt Sally serves the pie with cream
and we salve our wounds with the balm of family love.

But we are locked in tonight,
brothers and sisters behind bars
and only our thoughts can escape,
as the men with mirrors try to steal our souls.

With words we urge them to rise,
to rise up,
to push away the stone
and leave this place of darkness
like Jesus.

And rejoice,
on Easter morning.

"The Sure Cure for Anti-

is more information. Woman's suffrage is of more ancient lineage than most people think."

In pin curls and pearls we trample
the cookbooks and crochet hooks
in our path.
Undaunted by President Webb and
his band of mustachioed meddlers,
through the gates,
beyond the red brick wall,
we march with
gold sashes and bold banners.

The words of Rev. Shaw in our ears,
believing that the bold find favor
with fortune,
these brave women of Randolph-Macon
rally and raise hell,
because who else will?

"I have crouched too long by the little hearths at the bidding of Man, my mate—"

Miss Lucy Somerville
represents Randolph-Macon
at the National Equal Suffrage Convention
where presidents of two
women's colleges will speak and
"not less enjoyable will be the banquet for
college girls."

"New Zealand reports that her voting women are still beautiful"

Striding alongside her mother, Mrs. Nellie Nugent Somerville,
Lucy shakes the hand of President Wilson
(another president to be plied with civil words
and silver tongues).
Fine Southern ladies may balk and shudder,
but we will glory in being feminists.

When we have won our fair and equal rights
our daughters and sons will be free.

quotations from *The Sundial*, Randolph-Macon Woman's College student newspaper, 1915

And all because she wouldn't wash her hair

Lila refused—
absolutely refused—
to wash her hair.
With new tendrils sprouting down there,
(and sort of everywhere) she clung to her clothes like a liferaft.

I don't recognize my own self, she moaned.
I am not myself, she whimpered.
I'm someone else, she whispered.

The boys called her "Uncle Hank" behind her back,
but she heard
and still she wore her Dad's BVD white T
over her bathing suit all summer.
In the lake it puffed up like a roasted marshmallow
but Lila insisted.

With the river in her hair she swaggered up the dock
dripping teen angst like rain.
Saturday night was bath night, but Lila hid in her room
huddled up in a blanket reading Pippi Longstocking.
Pippi's grandfather was a kind man,
and her blazing braids never needed washing.

Come Sunday, she stayed home with Grandpa
listening to church bells chime
and a riled-up radio preacher.
When the boys returned clutching a goldfish from the fair,
wearing cotton candy smiles,
Lila fumed.

That fish set off a season of envy
and spiteful acts:
pilfered treats, broken bows, deflated balls,
taunted the boys daily.
Lila giggled.

Last out of the house and first in—
all summer the boys practiced a calculated vigilance—
they feared the fish was in mortal danger
(and they may have been right).

Lila lay in wait, patiently.

One cool morning as the sun rose and the chickens complained
an empty fishbowl leered,
the boys blubbered,

and Lila hummed in the shower.

Nail Polish Pollock

Gripped by toddler rage, blood pumping,
head pounding, heart thudding
indescribable ire
that comes on so sudden it nearly knocks you down,

she grabbed the bottle off the dresser and
twisted the cap with all her might.
Her strength, doubled by anger,
won out and soon she held the
tiny brush coated crimson
like crushed tomatoes, strawberry sauce, or cherry juice,
or blood.

The bedroom wall was white,
its bare surface beckoned.

A quick flick of the hand and it was done—
sharp spatters and strokes,
screaming what she couldn't speak.

She stood before her masterpiece,
staring, stunned,
riveted by the marks.

Her mother came,
saw stains glaring from the wall.
Then, there were other marks on a bare surface:
toddler bottom blooming red welts.

When her anger abated, replaced by jagged pain,
she grinned and said:

"It was worth it."

12 things I wish someone had told me before I gave birth

1. You will be ripped open and 2. your lips will never be the same 3. You won't use that candle you brought so the scent could distract you from the pain but 4. you will use the giant diaper pads to stanch the bleeding 5. Your father-in-law will try to enter the room just when the pain is most acute and 6. you will see his face gaping between your splayed knees 7. The nurses will count nine towels when the Doctor thought he used ten but 8. the Doctor will laugh triumphantly upon finding the tenth 9. A living being will be sucked out of you with a vacuum and 10. he will resemble a cone-head for the next week 11. He will scowl at you and the world with his swollen testicles and 12. you will smile at him through swollen eyes in a sterile room as his father sleeps awkwardly in a chair beside you.

Born and raised in upstate New York, **Jennifer L. Gauthier** has lived in Virginia for almost half her life. She has degrees from Vassar College, Wesleyan University and George Mason University. Since 2004, she has taught media, film and gender studies classes at Randolph College.

Her poems have appeared or are forthcoming in *Tiny Seed Literary Journal, South 85, Gyroscope Review, Nightingale & Swallow, River River, The Bookends Review*, little somethings press, *HerWords Magazine* and Tofu Ink Arts Press.

Her media commentary can be found online at the Pop Matters website, *The Critical Flame: A Journal of Literature and Culture and Mayday Magazine*, as well as in various academic journals. *naked: poems inspired by remarkable women*, was chosen as third runner-up in the 2020 New Women's Voices poetry competition sponsored by Finishing Line Press.

When not writing or reading, she loves to hike and bike with her husband and son and their dog.
Instagram: @jengauthierthinks

www.ingramcontent.com/pod-product-compliance
Lightning Source LLC
LaVergne TN
LVHW041518070426
835507LV00012B/1666